**For Annette
a remarkable Quaker lady.**

With thanks to:

Senja Brendon, Vember Brown, Tiree Dawson, Petra
Blahova, Tony Carden, Robert Leach, Kev Reynolds,
Heather May Rhodes, Jacqui Scott, Steve Scott,
Ro Thomas and Annie Truch

SUNLIGHT ON A FRAGMENTED ANXIOUS WORLD

COLIN MORTLOCK

ISBN 978-1-907362-04-0

What do you think of your experiences in wild Nature — those moments that were uplifting? They might well have been to do with beauty — from the tiniest flower to the starry universe — from a raindrop to an ocean view. Or they might have been to do with excitement and adrenalin — an adventure: kayaking, sailing, climbing, ballooning; or an unforgettable walk in an amazing place or in extreme conditions.

Whatever the range of your experiences, they are all related to the truth that you are elementally natural. After a lifetime in wild Nature, exploring my relationship with her, I know that what I have found is an ancient wisdom. This wisdom, if applied to how you live your life, will take you ever deeper into well-being — like sunlight on an anxious and fragmented world.

4 Lowther Gardens
Kents Bank Road
Grange over Sands
Cumbria
LA11 7EX

Tel: +44 (0) 1539 536522
colin@soadventure.org
www.soadventure.org

ISBN: 978-1-907362-04-0

A catalogue record of this book is available from The British Library.

Printed by H&H Reeds Printers Ltd.

CONTENTS

FOREWORD
by Satish Kumar

Colin Mortlock is a champion of wild Nature. He has dedicated all his life in celebration, conservation and promotion of the outdoors. He has walked 18,000 miles wondering and wandering in the magic of mountains, forests and lakes. During this long and rich pilgrimage he has experienced the unity of life. He has discovered the truth that people and nature are one. There is no separation or disconnection between the inner landscape and the outer landscape.

Now Colin has come up with the beautifully written book which you are holding in your hands. This is a book of immense importance in our modern world of materialism, industrialism and consumerism where we have created an illusion that nature is out there as a resource for the economy. Colin shatters that illusion and reminds us in no uncertain terms that nature is more than a resource; nature is the source of life itself. We misuse and abuse nature at our peril. We need to be reminded of this simple but forgotten truth and Colin has done so in an eloquent manner.

I recommend the book to the Reader not only to read it and cherish it but also implement the ideas and ideas expounded in this book by going out and by walking in nature, meditating on nature, embracing nature and becoming one with nature.

Satish Kumar
Editor Emeritus of Resurgence & Ecologist

INTRODUCTION

"All that man has eternally here, in multiplicity, is intrinsically one... This is the deepest depth."

Meister Eckhart 1260-1327

In 1992, I took early retirement from my post of Head of Outdoor Education at the Charlotte Mason College in Ambleside, the Lake District. Although I loved my work, I had become increasingly frustrated with the growing number of meetings concerned with money and bureaucracy. I had come to college to work with students in the outdoors and not to play politics.

For the next ten years, expeditions became my way of life — trekking in Scotland, the Alps, and the Pyrenees. Journeys were between one and three months. Annette, my wife, joined me when she was not teaching. Mostly I was solo. During this period, I walked over 18,000 miles along with considerable amounts of ascent.

The aims of the expeditions were to explore new areas and to find as many different types of wild flowers as possible. Over 30 years' experience of expeditions ensured I travelled as lightly and efficiently as possible. I was self-reliant with a tiny tent, minimal food and no phone. Every four days or so, I would descend into a valley and restock.

Somewhat to my surprise, on these expeditions I found a sense of well-being so powerful that such journeys seemed the ideal way of life. Key aspects that led to such positive feelings included:

Adventure – to plan a new route from a map and then to take that journey guaranteed an adventurous lifestyle. I did not search for specific adventures as I knew they would occur naturally. Being on my own intensified the whole experience.

Beauty – apart from my love of wild flowers, I had considerable interest in my surroundings. In addition to my basic concern for safety was the challenge of the wisdom: 'there is beauty in everything in Nature, if you can see it'. In addition, a magnifying glass opened up another world...

Hard work – days of 8–12 hours were often arduous, especially the long ascents from valley floor to passes and mountain summits. On many days, if the weather was dry, I would remove my footwear and sleep for up to 20 minutes before having a sparse lunch.

Simplicity – compared to living at home, my life was simpler and cheaper, and the rubbish from four days of wilderness travel was minimal. Yet in contrast to living in the urban world, the sense of well-being was far deeper.

Whilst all these aspects were key to my well-being, the major factor was that, despite being alone, I did not feel lonely. I gradually realised why and also that it had immense significance: **man is natural and is born to move naturally.** With my early morning starts, I merged into Nature and became part of her eternal rhythms. Most nights I would fall asleep within minutes. I felt Nature in all her forms was my friend. She would occasionally give me a good kick with a storm or other danger but I lived in unity with Nature. It was no wonder I was so content. I was now in no doubt that, elementally, **I was Nature.** (part of ..)

When you build something, it needs to be built on solid foundations. Failure to do so will inevitably lead to major problems, such as the collapse of the structure. The man-made world is no exception. Civilisation is collapsing because it is built on twin illusions:

- ## That we are separate from Nature
- ## That we are superior to Nature

Humankind urgently needs to be rebuilt on the wisdom that **We are Nature.** It is a vision based on love. The current human world is built on fear. My vision is of hope, joy, purity and freedom.

SUNLIGHT

We live in an increasingly complex, fragmented and troubled world. Unless we are particularly aware, then we also will tend to live in a fragmented, stressful and unnatural manner. David Bohm, a physicist writing in the 1980s, clearly saw its dangers:

"Throughout history, fragmentation has produced severe and destructive conflict on every level. This fragmentation ultimately may threaten the very existence of humanity."

Thirty years on, I have no doubt that we are very close to this crisis point. This publication, based essentially on reflection on experiences, provides an exciting way forward. It is based on the idea that **We are Nature**.

I have come to believe that this wisdom is true from reflection on a range of unusual experiences, mostly in wild Nature, along with extensive reading — ancient and modern, from East and West. This unity of man and Nature is an ancient wisdom:

"What is within us is without us. What is without us is within us."

The Upanishads

---

and from modern science:
"Every part of the universe contains the whole universe enfolded within it."

David Bohm

If anyone doubts the importance of this unity, remember your origins. Humans come from the unity of two people. Hopefully this is not simply a physical unity but a relationship based on love.

It may be worth considering moments in your life that have been extra-ordinary or special in a positive sense. Your memory will probably have recorded them in detail. They can happen at any time and anywhere. I would humbly suggest that all of them express the same elemental wisdom:

In the moment of the experience, you and the object of your attention are linked. Your separateness is suspended. You and the object have become a unity and there is a feel-good factor. These experiences can occur when you are doing something for which you have great enthusiasm — falling in love; intense experiences in the arts and music.[1]

We are Nature means each of us has phenomenal potential. The majority of that potential is creative rather than destructive. If we could realise it, wild Nature is startlingly good news for us. Mencius, the ancient Chinese philosopher, points the way:

"The tendency of man's nature to be good is like the tendency of water to flow downhill."

Nature gets on with the process of growing naturally — evolution. This means the human being is basically, naturally good. Only modern man in his shallow self-made urban world has allowed badness and corruption to dominate.

1. See Appendix for further comments.

THE MAN-MADE WORLD

Imagine you can experience the detail of the entire history of the human race. When you do that, you realise the obvious: your feelings have taken a huge destructive hit. You know that in the comparatively short space of time man has been on the planet, he has caused havoc, brought destruction to the earth itself and almost all life forms, including his own species.

You applaud the remarkable diversity and range of human achievements but you can see the overall human record has been disgraceful. As someone who read and studied history, and as a member of the human race, I, for one, am deeply ashamed.

Just in my lifetime, we have allowed materialism, instant convenience and immediate gratification to contaminate almost all corners of the planet. Rampant consumerism is now a more powerful force than any previous or current religion. The quality of an individual has become defined by what they own. Having has become more important than being.

Alongside this has developed rampant corruption. With the Freedom of Information Act in 2000, we began to see the sickening levels of corruption from the scandal of MPs' expenses to the 2008 financial crisis and beyond. The following may sum up the attitude of some of the key players:

"I, as a top financier, deserve my million-pound bonus for this year, for life is about money and I am an expert. You may not approve. Tough. I have the power and status to do what I want. It is unfortunate, of course, about the recession and all those in poverty, but they are not directly my concern."

We live in a world of increasing specialisation. Pulitzer prize winner Chris Hedges, author of the bestseller, *Empire of Illusion*, and journalist for the New York Times on various war fronts, explains why this is a problem:

"The specialised dialect and narrow education of doctors, academics, economists, social scientists, military officers, investment bankers and government bureaucrats keeps each sector locked in its narrow role. The over-arching structure of the corporate state and the idea of the common good are irrelevant to specialists. They exist to make the system work, not to examine it."

As a result a tiny minority largely control what happens in the man-made world. Some control corporations which operate in a moral void and define progress in terms of maximising profit. This minority is extremely clever and ruthless. For these individuals to be effective, they require largely compliant and confused populations. They also need a system of propaganda and a mass media that offers a maximum of spectacle and entertainment. The result is that we now have **celebrity cultures.** In such societies, good character, which traditionally was so important, has been replaced by the vices of loudness and egotism coupled with an attitude of success at any price.

I remember the words of Charles Birch, the eminent Australian scientist:

> *"Too often, man is after power, prestige, and social approval. Egoistic corruption of universal ideals is a persistent fact."*

A central aim of government is the security of the citizens. At first sight this aim seems fine. We all want to feel safe as we move around. Those who wield the major power, however, exploit this aim unscrupulously to further their own selfish ends. The result is that most countries, including America, Russia, Germany, France, Britain and China, have deliberately based their economies on military might and aggression. These are societies based on fear and anxiety, not on love and unity.

Consider the wisdom of Confucius:

> *"That state is the worst governed which has the most laws. That state is the best governed which has the least laws. The perfect state has no laws."*

What has gone wrong? We have allowed those in power, local to global, either through their ignorance or their deliberate actions, to perpetuate the illusion that we are all separate from, and superior to, wild Nature. This illusion urgently needs replacing by the truth: We are Nature. Despite the fact

that there are good people everywhere, the modern world is essentially corrupt. In practice, it is ruled by money, status and power — by the vices rather than the virtues. As a direct result of that corruption and use of vices, humans now face formidable problems including:

- Global warming / climate change
- Destructive weather worldwide...any time...anywhere
- Pollution of our air, water, soils and bodies
- Economic, financial and social extremism
- Obesity and its consequences
- Overpopulation
- Trivialisation (dumbing down)

The stark truth is that most of these problems are becoming increasingly serious.

THE INNER JOURNEY

*"The most important journey is
the journey inwards."*

Dag Hammarskjöld

In the last section, I emphasised that the man-made world is corrupted and now faces serious global problems. That world is made up of individuals and to effect change requires the efforts of each of us.

My search for truth — the inner journey — took me back to basics. One way to start is to ask oneself:

Who Am I?
Where am I going?
How do I get there?

WHO AM I?

Like every daisy, pebble and snowflake, I am unique. **But** beneath that separateness there is a unity with Nature. A major clue to that unity is our **sameness**. For example, we are natural. We come from and return to Nature and we are governed by natural forces such as instincts. All of us seek contentment.

We have the same aspects. These include:

Physical — the body: its condition affects everything else.

Mental — our intellect: the home of our thinking.

Emotional – our feelings: shallow and deep, positive and negative. The central ones are **fear and love.**

Spiritual – by far the most mysterious. Physically it does not appear to exist. Yet since at least the time of the Greeks, from the classic writings of both East and West, there is agreement of its huge importance. To deny its existence is to deny the wisdom of the ages.

All my actions depend on what I value. My values are based on my use of virtues and vices. The spirit therefore is the home of my virtues and vices that, in turn, determines whether my actions are good or bad, positive or negative.

We need to be aware that within the self there is the Shadow. This is the dark or negative side of the personality – home of the vices. Within this shadow lies potentially the most dangerous enemy – the **ego.** It surrounds conscious self, protects your uniqueness, and emphasises your separateness. If you allow it to grow beyond self-respect then it quickly dominates. The ego then incessantly demands gratification. If you allow this to happen, then arrogance is the only destination. In a world ruled by money, status and power, it is commonplace. It is divisive and the direct opponent of love and unity.

> **Egotism is no less than the psychological cancer of the materialistic world.**

Having crudely divided a person into various bits, I need to stress that, in practice, we are a whole person in which everything is not only interlinked but everything affects everything else. Bruce Lipton, a scientist from the new field of epigenetics, declares that each of us is composed of around 50 trillion cells. Each cell can take its own action in terms of what is best for the individual (see *The Biology of Belief* 2005).

WHERE AM I GOING?

I refer here not just to my immediate aims but to my whole life. Beneath the often consumer-driven shallow aims (e.g. convenient lifestyle, fun and enjoyment, sex, shopping, instant fame) are deeper aims. Throughout history there have been searches for the meaning of human existence – to do with concepts like Truth, Beauty, Freedom, Wisdom and Happiness.

The following is a simple answer to this question:

> **I am going towards fulfilment of my positive potential – in all senses of being human.**
>
> **This means striving towards intellectual, physical, emotional, and spiritual maturity – a lifelong process.**

HOW DO I GET THERE?

The modern world can be a highly desirable and exciting place. It is also complex, dangerous and corrupting. In practice, a materialistic society encourages the worship of money and power, status and selfishness. It encourages *wanting* not being. With its clever advertising, it is relentless. There is no hiding place. To fight this corruption and evil, you have two magnificent forces for goodness within you: the **virtues** and the **wisdoms**. On the other hand you also have your Shadow, the potentially massive force of evil or badness in the form of all the **vices**. Where good meets bad, where virtues / wisdoms confront vices, is the **conscience** – your conscience.

It is common sense to regard the conscience as the battlefield between the good and the bad. If you accept this ideal, then you have solved — at least in theory — what William James, the philosopher expressed succinctly:

"The problem of man is to find a moral substitute for war."

In war you give of your best because your survival depends upon it, but war is destructive, not creative.

It seems highly sensible to regard this war as a lifelong process within ourselves, in our conscience. Our freedom is that we choose between our positive and negative aspects in all the billions of decisions we make. Life is choice — each time we make a positive decision, we grow towards fulfilling our potential and experience feelings of well-being. Making negative decisions stunts and twists our growth.

At the core of being human lies the choice of action between the character strengths, the virtues, and the weaknesses, the vices. The truth that 'We are Nature' implies most strongly that we try to live by the former. 'We are Nature' also implies that we accept joyously what lies behind such words as love, beauty, peace, wisdom and, not least, purity.

Some virtues and opposing vices:

Honesty --- Dishonesty

Awareness --- Ignorance

Respect --- Disrespect

Compassion --- Indifference

Determination --- Irresolution

Patience --- Impatience

Self-discipline --- Indiscipline

Self-reliance --- Dependence

Concentration --- Distraction

Unselfishness --- Selfishness

Empathy --- Self-centredness

Friendliness --- Unfriendliness

Kindness --- Unkindness

Gentleness --- Harshness

Gratitude --- Ingratitude

Tolerance --- Intolerance

Forgiveness --- Condemnation

Justice --- Injustice

Humour --- Humourlessness

Creativity --- Destructiveness

Responsibility --- Irresponsibility

Humility --- Arrogance

Purity --- Impurity

Simplicity --- Complexity

Vitality --- Apathy

Courage --- Cowardice

The baseline virtue has to be honesty with oneself. To be ruthlessly honest in deciding on what action to take, and on reflecting on that experience, is essential. It needs to become the strongest of habits. It may help to visualise your conscience as your moral or psychological spine. Like your spine, it needs to be upright and strong.

Gandhi underlines the challenge:

"I have only three enemies: my favourite enemy is the British Empire, my second enemy, the Indian people, is far more difficult, but my most formidable opponent is a man named Mahatma Gandhi. With him, I seem to have very little influence."

The quality or calibre of a person is dependent essentially on how they live the detail of their life rather than their accomplishments, important though these may be. That quality is seen by their consistent use of the virtues and defines their character.

How we grow depends on the quality of our experiences balanced by the quality of our reflections on them. Like the seed of the oak, we have the potential to become a giant oak or not to bother and become a stunted and twisted specimen.

THE WISDOMS

If the purpose of our complex journey through life is to seek positive fulfilment – physically, emotionally, mentally, and spiritually – then we need all the help we can get. A major source of assistance is wisdom. But what is wisdom? Here are some hints:

Carl Jung: *"The wisdom of the unconscious."*
Accept that you have an unconscious, a deeper self.

Proverb: *"Experience is the mother of wisdom."*
You learn by action – **by doing**.

Meister Eckhart: *"A life of wisdom must be a life of contemplation combined with action."*
Evaluate your 'doing' with honesty (virtue) and awareness (virtue).

Bertrand Russell: *"To conquer fear is the beginning of wisdom."*
Fears are with you throughout life – your positive growth comes from confronting them.

Ralph Waldo Emerson: *"Wisdom has its roots in goodness."*
Annette (my wife) lived a life of goodness, was recognised for her wisdom and died happy.

- -

Aristotle regarded wisdom as excellence. Study different types of wisdom and bring them into your active life at every opportunity. To become wise is the highest of accolades. The virtue of humility is a core characteristic.

In use, wisdom is a character strength expressing expertise in the conduct and meaning of life. Here are a few examples:

- Learning is a lifelong experience.

- Life as an endless search for truth - an approach of humility.

- Aim to live in each moment with vitality.

- Quality of experiences to be balanced by quality of reflection on those events.

- A life of balance brings well-being.

- Life as a search for beauty - within and without.

- An increasing sense of awe and wonder.

- Realising everything in Nature is dynamic – including all aspects of oneself.

- Heroes and heroines as inspiration – past, present and within oneself.

- Creative energy as eternal delight.

- Look to others for their strengths – look to self for weakness.

- Unity is integrity is love.

- The most important thing is to die at the right time.

PERSONAL EXPERIENCES LEADING TO UNITY & 'WE ARE NATURE'

At the start of this book I used solo trekking expeditions after I had taken early retirement to confirm the major discovery of my life: the ancient wisdom that 'We are Nature'. If someone had said that to me as a young man, I would have thought that they were mad. I knew I was separate and never was that felt so strongly as when I thought I was going to fall off when leading a rock climb.

My three years teaching at Manchester Grammar School (MGS) coincided with my decision to give up climbing as my major adventure activity and take up canoeing. I soon learnt basic kayaking skills and gradually became efficient at tackling river rapids. On one trip to Mid Wales to paddle the Vyrnwy Gorge, after a fortnight of almost continuous rain, I had an epic. My knowledge of the river was confined solely to the study of a map. Fellow paddler Steve Schaeffer, school captain, was fearless but even less experienced than I. Annette, my wife, was our driver. The first mistake was to ignore the minibus and canoe trailer driving away from the river. I discovered later that this vehicle contained experienced canoeists from Birmingham Canoe Club who had inspected the gorge and decided it was suicidal. The second mistake was our inspection of the start of the gorge from 50 metres above it. There were no rocks, just waves of brown and white and a roar of noise. I did not know that the size of the waves couldn't be appreciated from above. Once in our kayaks, we set off and immediately became committed to a giant dipper – a maelstrom of brown water, flecked with white. My mind flashed back to the guidebook description of the highest difficulty of white water:

"cannot be attempted without risk to life."

My climbing background took over – total concentration – this is it... no time for terror – adrenalin in full flow. Then I was wiped out where a flooded side river met the maelstrom I was riding. Somehow I just managed to roll, only to see Steve, who was following, get wiped out at the same place. He failed to roll, and worse, once he surfaced, he let go of his upturned boat. I knew I had to rescue him as soon as possible as we were only at the top end of the gorge. He was well built, tall and heavy. Somehow I found the strength to tow him to the bank. He then scrambled out. I found his kayak a quarter of a mile downstream stuck in a tree.

Looking back on this incident I believe the strength I found to rescue him came from my depths. I knew I could not face his parents, with whom Annette and I had dined. I believe this strength came from 'We are Nature', a concept of which I was ignorant at that time.

After MGS I moved to Glasbury on Wye to become the first Warden of the Woodlands Outdoor Centre – a residential centre for the city of Oxford and its schools. Living by the river as well as kayaking on it all year round for six years led me to learn to love the river. Like a human being its moods were infinitely variable and moved from one extreme to the other. In a good summer it was often rocky, shallow and beautiful. In winter it was often in spate. Occasionally it would flood demanding great respect if kayaking on its tumultuous ride. Once it had a six-metre flood – so powerful that it became the first item on the national news. This was because below Hereford there was extensive flooding. On that day the kayaking staff and their young group of 14-year-olds left their kayaks at the Centre and took the minibus to view the river's splendour. A sense of awe and wonder was the order of the day..

Another particular memory is also relevant in my journey towards unity with Nature. The incident was unexpected and all the more memorable for that. The river was in spate and I was attempting something new — a 16-mile paddle **up** the river from Glasbury to Builth Wells. I was alone and hoped to do it without getting out of the boat before the finish.

It took place on a cold, bright day in the winter of 1969–70 and I saw no one whilst on the river.

Sitting in an eddy resting before tackling the crux of a rapid, I noticed a shadow beneath the kayak: it was a large salmon. I sensed my affinity with this magnificent fish. In order to complete my journey successfully, I had to think like a salmon. Not only that but I had to try to use my skills as efficiently as the fish. Like the fish, I rested in the eddies (calm pools) and then had to execute the least tiring way up the broken water. What the salmon did naturally had taken me years of hard practice. It was difficult not to feel humility. My journey was a mere 16 miles. The salmon had probably come from Greenland!

In summer, with rivers often low, surfing on the coast became the attraction. From my home at Glasbury on Wye, surf kayaking at Newgale in Pembrokeshire and Rhossili Bay on the Gower were weekly events for work and during holiday times. Our surfing expressed the music of the Beach Boys. Eventually, up to three-metre-high waves were ridden — forwards and backwards and then end-over-end. Eskimo rolling radically improved. Riding a wave knowing that you were part of it was exhilarating. Each wave was different and skills needed to be fine-tuned. It still seems to me to be one of the best examples of joy from being at one with Nature. This must be especially significant if it is true that the human race originally came from the sea.

It was inevitable that I would eventually explore beyond the surf by kayak. Kayaking along coastlines and around islands became a passion and, gradually, doing such journeys solo became a major occupation.

A particularly memorable trip was a solo night crossing of 40 miles from the Lake District to the Isle of Man. On a June evening in 1981 I had set off west through a small surf. Paddling into the sunset had felt surreal, yet warm and exciting. Around four hours later I reckoned I was about halfway, only my mood had changed. The sun had been replaced by grey darkness. There was no sign of land or life in any direction. I felt very lonely, tense and gloomy. A large bank of sea fog immediately to the south did not help. Suddenly I had a visitor – a tiny bird. It seemed to be curious and stayed several minutes. I realised I was privileged to see my first storm petrel – the tiniest of the sea birds weighing a mere 28g – more like a butterfly than a bird as it fluttered around me. Then it vanished. I continued following a compass bearing westward into the night, but my mood had changed. My gloom had been replaced by warm and positive feelings again. The loneliness had disappeared. With dawn came a cool northeasterly breeze and a choppy sea. I did not mind and, in good spirits, landed on Ramsay beach at 0430. The trip had taken 8 hours. I later realised that meeting the storm petrel had been what Maslow called a "peak experience". It was to be an important step in understanding my relationship to Nature.

We learn most from our own experiences. There is no substitute. At the age of 45, in 1981, I returned to Sitka in Alaska to begin a solo sea kayak expedition northbound on the

Pacific towards Anchorage. Two years previously, a friend and I had completed a 1,200km expedition from Prince Rupert north to Sitka. I fell in love with Alaska and its coastline. The contrast with the man-made world could not have been more extreme:

- Three environments met: massive forests, mountains up to 4600 metres and the Pacific Ocean.

- Human beings were rare.

- No pollution — the coastline was pristine in contrast to even the most remote beaches in Britain which are covered in oil, plastic and other debris.

After this first trip, I decided I would return and therefore I would leave my boat in Sitka. On Friday, 1st July 1981, I began the solo journey. I was not in the happiest of moods. The weather was poor and I had learnt in Sitka that two solo kayakers had died in separate incidents in the area the previous year — eaten by bears. That I carried no gun did not help.

The expedition lasted a month and I covered 1,000km. A summer of bad weather ruled out Anchorage. Instead I explored Glacier Bay. Inevitably there were adventures of all kinds. Close encounters with whales and sea lions, for example, proved exciting. Each night, I had to land and pitch my tiny tent — either on the edge of, or in, the forest. Normal days on the water were between eight and twelve hours. If I was lucky, I landed once a day for lunch. Several times, however, I had lunch in the boat due to a bear waiting on the beach where I intended to land.

After the first few days of the expedition something happened psychologically that had never happened before and has never happened again. Each time I went back to the ocean, providing there were no immediate dangers that demanded attention, I started going into my unconscious. This carried on throughout the trip but only when on the water. What was staggering was how deep I went — to depths I did not know existed. The only comparison I could make is falling in love with another person. I had always regarded that experience as both joyous and of depth. This ocean experience was neither joyous nor just deep. It was so deep that it left me in a state of awe. It made no difference, however, to the practical adventure of the expedition in that I felt no psychological security. My fears remained throughout the journey such were the dangers. On returning home, all I knew was that there was something here that was way more mysterious and important than adrenalin adventure.[2]

Over the next few years, I found my reflections on that trip kept coming back to the same thing — the depth of going into my unconscious was so huge that it had to be an oceanic experience.

In simple terms: the ocean was within me.

Obviously, in a rational sense, this was rubbish. In a psychological sense, it was possible. The spirit has no finite boundaries. It is infinite.

Although I did not realise it at the time, I had taken a significant step towards knowing that 'We are Nature.'

Then, in the late 1980s, there occurred another unusual experience. It was a summer morning, and I had gone to check out a new rock scramble in a rarely visited ravine in the Lake District. At the foot of the climb, I noticed a solitary tall plant with striking dark blue flowers. My attitude to flowers up to

---

2. It was only in 2015 that I realised why I had gone into my unconscious: I was seeking relief from my fears and there was nowhere else to go.

that time had been one of contempt. Flowers were something for the ladies. I did the climb. Almost unbelievably, at the top, was one more flower of the same type. I knew then that I had to find out what it was — though I had never before had such a desire. Annette was a keen botanist and quickly gave me the answer: *Aquilegia vulgaris*, the Eagle flower and the State flower of Colorado.

Up to that point in my life my status and self-respect were bound up with my expertise as an adventurer. Dangerous adventure is self-centred, inevitably, because your life is under threat. Out of nowhere had come a sudden passion for wild flowers. After that initial experience with the columbine my major enthusiasm for the next couple of years was trying to find as many wild flowers as possible in northern Britain. I later realised this unexpected development was a major step towards discovering I was Nature. My egotism took a massive hit. Overnight I had become an enthusiastic amateur botanist who faced major difficulties as a non-scientist, trying to identify what I had found. Without accurate identification I could not get to know the flowers. The thrill of adrenalin was replaced by the joy of finding and then discovering a flower's identity. In addition, with a hand lens, I began to appreciate the wondrous beauty of plants.

Expeditions to the Alps and the Pyrenees, along with wild coastlines were eventually to provide both physical adventure and beautiful wild flowers. In that process, encouraged by being solo for much of the time, I sense I became less arrogant and more mature. Over succeeding years my enthusiasm for flowers has broadened, from wild flowers only, to garden flowers and indoor plants.

During the period of solo expeditions immediately after retirement, an unexpected experience occurred that was to become a key feature of the concept 'We are Nature.'

In 1998, I was invited to give a keynote talk in Auckland to the third National Outdoor Education Conference of New Zealand. The talk was based on a sudden thought that I scribbled down when I sat with a blank sheet of A4 wondering on what to base my talk. This is what I scribbled:

"Everything in Nature is alive in its own way, is on its own adventure and deserves its own well-being. Everything in Nature from a grain of sand to a star, from the tiniest flower to a human being, is of no more and no less importance than anything else."

This thought became known as 'The Wilderness Message'. To my surprise and delight, the talk was warmly received and I was set up with an impromptu lecture tour the length of the country.

The Wilderness Message is a central tenet of my philosophy. This Message should be the basis of a Universal Value Framework for humankind.

It indicates that:

- **No human being is any more or less important than any other human being; and**

- **No human being is more important than anything else in Nature.**

> **The Message implies that, using our common sense, each of us lives with minimal destruction to our surroundings. This is a message of peace.**

Accepting the Wilderness Message also underlines the elemental importance of the virtues of justice (fairness) and humility. Over the years, I have asked both individuals and groups, especially when out in Nature, to react spontaneously to the Wilderness Message. Most respond positively. I was later to realise that the Wilderness Message had not only come from deep within me but that it was during my 10-year period of solo expeditions. I know we are shaped by our surroundings. I do not regard it as too fanciful to maintain that wild Nature was using me as a voice to the man-made world.

ANNETTE

For nearly 50 years, Annette had been my wife. In 2002, now retired from teaching, she completed three one-month trekking expeditions with me in Spain, Crete, and the Ariège region of the Pyrenees. At 64, her fitness for such arduous journeys was impressive. In May the following year, she died of bowel cancer. Shocked and depressed, I was only partially relieved by her insistence that, in her final weeks in a hospice, she was in a 'bubble of happiness'.

As well as being the mother of our three daughters, she was a science teacher, at both primary and secondary levels. She was blessed with considerable intelligence and the widest of interests. Eventually she became a Quaker. Her vitality was matched by her unselfishness. After her demise I went and lived remotely in Scotland. In trying to understand her values, I eventually rang her headmistress. She asked me how I was, to which I replied "very depressed". She then told me off. Did I not realise how lucky I had been to have Annette as my partner? She then said, "Everyone, pupils and staff in both schools, loved Annette".

I later read in *The Oxford Book of Death*, "How you die depends on how you live the detail of your life".

I recalled Annette had loved almost all human beings and had loved wild Nature in its entirety, including slugs and worms. I then realised why Annette had been happy in death.

Her life, and how she faced death, was inspirational. She beautifully demonstrated the elemental importance of living a life of goodness, vitality and courage. She had lived a life of goodness by living unselfishly and in each moment. I sense that she would have had no problem accepting that we are Nature. It came to me soon after her death that, if all those in positions of power — from local to global, had lived their lives with the same principles as she had, then the man-made world would not be facing many of its current perils.

"Love is the general name of the quality of attachment and it is capable of infinite degradation and is the source of our greatest errors; but when it is even partially refined, it is the energy and passion of the soul in the search for Good, the force that joins us to Good, and joins us to the world through Good. Its existence is that unmistakeable sign that we are spiritual creatures, attracted by excellence and made for the Good. It is a reflection of the warmth and light of the sun."

Iris Murdoch

The link between LOVE and the VIRTUES/VICES

After her death I had problems linking her values with mine. She had lived a life of love (goodness). Extensive reading left me in no doubt that:

> **Love in its universal sense is the most important word in any language.**

In my personal life and work in adventure education I had used ten virtues. Then a friend suggested that I look at St. Paul's second letter to the Corinthians. In it Paul describes nine components of love. Eight of these were on my list of key virtues:

Patience	Kindness
Generosity	Sincerity
Humility	Unselfishness
Vitality	Courtesy

I then came across this quotation:

"Why love among the virtues is not known,
is that love is them all, contract in one."

John Donne

The link became obvious and the wisdom of Donne was more than helpful. Love in its universal and positive sense is the unity (oneness) and all the virtues are parts of that unity. Love is the positive circle and each virtue is a segment of that circle.

At the same time we need to remember our Shadow. Again I see a circle — the negative circle — in which each vice is a segment of that circle. Egotism — narcissism — self-centredness reside here.

We contain both circles. All the virtues and vices lie dormant within us until used.

CHARACTERISTICS OF ANY CIVILISED SOCIETY

Like Einstein, Professor Whitehead had deep concern for the human world. In 1933, he published *Adventures of Ideas*, in which he suggested that there were five characteristics of any civilised society:

ART

BEAUTY

PEACE

TRUTH

ADVENTURE

Modern societies, I would suggest, tend to be characterised by their opposites:

Ugly art not beautiful art

Ugliness not Beauty

War not Peace

Lies not Truth

Misadventure not adventure

Wild Nature, on the other hand, often demonstrates his five characteristics.

Art I see as demonstrating the spiritual and sacred. The canvas of Nature leaves me with a sense of awe and wonder at the artist who created such magnificence.

Beauty is everywhere in wild Nature. The more the awareness, macro and micro, the more beauty there is to see.

Peace and quiet are characteristic of so much of wild Nature. Feelings of timelessness are common. Eternal rhythms are to be experienced in contrast to the frenetic pace and noise of the modern world.

Truth- when I adventured on the rock face and mountain, on river and ocean; when I was on the edge of my capabilities, I was facing the truth of the matter: the natural examination I had set myself. In other words, was I up to the challenge?

Adventure- Whitehead wrote, *"Without adventure, civilisation is in full decay"*.

BRINGING IT TOGETHER

*"Nothing in this world is as powerful as
an idea whose time has come."*

Victor Hugo

In thinking about what to put in this summary, a word
jumped impishly into my mind: smile – a small word with
the knock-out punch of a world champion boxer. I cannot
think of a better word with its power to reduce friction
and tension. Literally priceless, it encourages the positive
nature of being human. It is a characteristic of the virtues
of friendliness, kindness, gentleness, gratitude and humour.

I smile because I know I have had an extremely fortunate
life having spent most of it in wild Nature – that supreme
University of the Wilderness. Initially I was drawn by the
excitement of adventurous activities – the climbing, kayaking
and sailing in particular. With hindsight I can see that
survival and enthusiasm demanded some of the virtues –
determination, patience, concentration, self-reliance, self-
discipline – to name a few.

Then came the solo sea kayak expedition in Alaska (1981) that
left me in a state of awe and wonder. There was something
in this majestic and pristine wonderland that was way beyond
adrenalin adventure. I became a pilgrim adventurer. By the
year 2000 or thereabouts, in my early 60s, I knew, without
the slightest of doubts, what it was: **I was Nature.**

Extensive reading and understanding what was so special
about Annette – her smile even amidst her deep physical
suffering towards the end – plus the ultimate importance of

the word love, in its universal sense, has given me something of the truth of what humankind needs to do if it is to have a civilized future.

That something urgently needs to be done cannot be seriously doubted. Despite the fact that there are good people everywhere, the modern world is corrupt. In practice it is ruled by money, status and power, by the vices rather than the virtues.

We live in a world dominated by science, technology and intellectualism. This world can often make our feelings seem comparatively unimportant. Yet our feelings go to the core of our being. They need to be recognised as of major importance. Ultimately I regard my feelings as more important than my thinking. I know I am Nature because I have felt it.

Duane Elgin, writing in the 1980s in *Beyond Ego* puts his finger on the problem:

"We are engaged in a race between self-destruction and self-discovery."

---

30 years on from when he made that comment, I sense that we urgently need to win that race. To bring his sentence into 2016, I would lengthen it:

"We are engaged in a race between self-destruction, through egotism and fragmentation, and the self-discovery that beneath our uniqueness, there is an underlying unity – we are Nature."

Radical problems demand radical solutions. Nothing could be more radical than changing one's attitude from "I am separate from and superior to, wild Nature" to "I am Nature". Your uniqueness, of course, remains but embracing this wisdom of unity brings great news — you have magnificent potential. It really is up to you in terms of how far and to what extent you grow — physically, emotionally, mentally and spiritually — towards well-being. The more you live by the virtues, the more you will grow positively. There is also the comfort of the wisdom of the Wilderness Message — that no-one is any more or less important than you are and that we should all try to live with minimal destruction to our natural surroundings.

Unless we move towards a man-made world based on love and a universal-values framework of the character strengths then humankind has no civilized future. Nor does it deserve one. Einstein the brilliant scientist points the way:

"A human being is a part of the whole called by us 'the universe'. He experiences himself, his thoughts and feelings as something separate from the rest — a kind of optical delusion of his consciousness. This delusion is a kind of prison for us, restricting us to our personal desires and affection for a few persons nearest to us. Our task must be to free ourselves from this prison by widening our circle of understanding and compassion to embrace all living creatures and the whole of nature in its beauty."

Let's see if we can make Einstein smile.

THE WAY FORWARD: THE FOUNDATION

The quotation by Victor Hugo at the start of the previous chapter:

*"Nothing is so powerful as an idea
whose time has come"*

is only true if that idea becomes a powerful reality. If it does not then it is useless, especially at a time when human civilisation is about to go over the edge of a cliff.

In 2009, I published *The Spirit of Adventure*, but was already beginning to realise that books alone were inadequate if one wished to see radical change in a corrupt world. My shelves were rapidly filling up with such books. Thus, in 2010, the Spirit of Adventure Foundation (SOAF) was established. Its vision is:

To influence modern societies to become a global civilisation based on love and unity with Nature.

The Foundation celebrates and promotes all that is positive and worthwhile about being human. It aims to bring together all the positive fragments of human endeavour and creativity into an organic whole. This broadest of aims is critically important if humankind is to have a civilised future.

SOAF:

- Is based on ideals of integrity, beauty, peace and love

- Embraces the urgent need for humanity to live by all the virtues

- Proposes the Wilderness Message as the basis for living in harmony with Nature

- Proposes environmental awareness, pure adventure, and expeditions for all young people

- Has Satish Kumar as a principal adviser (www.resurgence.org/satish-kumar)

- Sees learning as a lifelong process

- Is free and open to all ages

Is SOAF really necessary?

YES – a resounding YES

There are millions of individuals, groups and NGOs who strive to live positively and leave the world a better place for future generations. Unfortunately, whilst they achieve a great deal, they cannot win the war against rampant consumerism. This is because they are fragmented.

Even Greenpeace, the World Wildlife Fund and Friends of the Earth are fragments. Admittedly they are large fragments with over 10 million supporters. In 2011 all three Chief Executive Officers came together on the BBC World Service and said,

---

"We are winning very significant battles but we are losing the planet".

What they meant was that even with their combined incor of $1 billion, they had no hope against the might of rampant materialism. $30 billion was earned by one oil company, Exxon Mobil, in 2011. Such giants have massive advertising power, saying something like 'hey folks, not to worry about environmental concerns, it is business as usual. Carry on and enjoy life.'

What this means is simply that rampant materialism and the tiny unscrupulous minority who steer it, will continue to dominate unless SOAF becomes tens of millions strong and has the major relevant organisations enthusiastically in support. This is an almighty challenge but success is essential. The alternative is Armageddon.

The current threat of global climate change is real and increasingly threatening. Unless all the positive fragments come together, through something like SOAF, then humankind has no chance of even restraining the materialistic technological monster.

Individually we are the tiniest of fragments. How can our individual actions possibly affect the rest of the human race? My answer is simple: We Are Nature – each of us. Therefore each of us needs to come together – through joining SOAF – to become a free global unifying organisation. By making that decision and encouraging your friends to join – you take the path to feelings of well-being.

The Foundation currently has over 500 members from 20 countries. It is in its infancy and is a dynamic ship that must be steered by its members.

Let's make the Foundation the greatest expedition the world has ever seen.

Please see the website: **www.soadventure.org**

HISTORICAL SUPPORT FOR SOAF

Not only is the spirit the most important aspect of any individual, the spirit never dies. Quite apart from Annette's spirit being strongly present in my life after she had physically departed, there were other human spirits. I have been very conscious of some of these exemplars. Across the global stage, bestride people like Mahatma Gandhi, Albert Schweitzer, and Doctor Edward Wilson of polar fame. Then there are those famous environmentalists who knew about their unity with Nature: in America, John Muir, Aldo Leopold, and Rachel Carson for example; in the UK, in the Lake District, the Romantic Movement — Wordsworth, Coleridge, Keats, Shelley — Ruskin and more recently John Wyatt. All of these and so many other kindred spirits, speak to me from my bookshelves. I sense their strong, if invisible, support for what I am trying to do.

I feel that there would also be support from the millions of individuals in history who lived creatively and peacefully.

There are further untold millions who died in war who fought in the hope of a better, less destructive human world.

POSTSCRIPT

Please allow me a postscript — one word again: beauty.
John Keats, one of the Romantic poets, wrote:

"...Beauty is truth, truth Beauty...that is all ye know on earth and all ye need to know."

I interpret that as seeing:

Beauty in one's surroundings — from micro to macro

Beauty in terms of human contact and relationships

Beauty in terms of one's own thoughts and actions

I would tentatively suggest we make John Keats smile by naming what we are about as:

THE NEW ROMANTIC MOVEMENT

If it does take off big time, then the earth will painfully smile as well; although we do not have time on our side.

APPENDIX - THE POSSIBILITY THAT WE ARE NATURE

I am convinced that most people have the capacity to experience unity with Nature. Reflect on your own unusual experiences — those that gave you warm feelings — and then consider whether they could have had that message of unity, of not feeling completely alone. Here are three types:

Moments of Synchronicity (C. J. Jung)
Peak Experiences (A.H. Maslow)
Flow (M. Csikszentmihalyi)

Please do not say that there is no proof of unity. You do not need scientific proof if you know something from your feelings. This wisdom has been around for a long time. For example:

"I and all things in the universe are one."

Chuang-Tzu (4BC)...

In the 1980s, Norway witnessed a major environmental protest in the far north. The government proposed to build a hydroelectric dam on the main river to provide electricity from which the locals would benefit. The local Laplanders fiercely objected. When asked why, their reply was:

"Never, the river here is part of us."

There have been large-scale events — music festivals, concerts and sporting events — where everyone (spectators and performers) has been engulfed by unity.

Here is a relevant quotation from the renowned monk, Thich Nhat Hanh (a man proposed for the Nobel Peace Prize by Martin Luther King):

"We have to remember that our body is not limited to what lies within the boundary of our skin. Our body is much more immense. If the sun were to stop shining the flow of our life would stop. The sun is our second heart...it gives all life on earth the warmth necessary for existence...all of us — people, animals, plants, and minerals — consume the sun directly and indirectly. We cannot begin to describe all the effects of the sun, that great heart outside of our body."